It Happened To Me

By
Josephine Woods

ISBN: 1-905451-23-7

A CIP catalogue for this book is available from the National Library.

Printed in Ireland

This book was published in cooperation with
Choice Publishing & Book Services Ltd, Ireland
Tel: 041 9841551 Email: info@choicepublishing.ie
www.choicepublishing.ie

Dedication

I dedicate this book to the precious memory of my wonderful, toil worn and self-sacrificing mother who left this world on the 08th September 1965. As the book tells you, dear reader, just a few short months after her passing she returned to use me as a channel of consolation to ease the pain in the grieving hearts of the family she left behind, the little family she so dearly loved. Her precious words to me, in reply to my excited question, "Mother, this is wonderful, where have you been?" will remain in my memory as long as I am on this earth. So often they come back to comfort me whenever I'm feeling down and sad. To me her thrilling, memorable words, her enlightening and thought-provoking reply, "here, beside you all the time!", they are the elixir of my life. My soul is filled with gratitude to this unique, loving and courageous mother of mine, stretching our from beyond the grave to tell me that she is still with me. This earth life was for her a vale of tears, a life full of hardship, physical pain and keen disappointment. If the expression of joy on her countenance that I was so blessed and privileged to see is anything to go by, then without doubt she has indeed found her well-deserved 'heaven'.

My dear, unselfish and unforgettable mother I salute you and in this factual book of mine so sincerely, dedicated to you I thank you.

Your daughter
Josephine

" Seek and Ye shall Find"

This I Did – I Sought – Then

It Happened to Me

Introduction:

This book, except for its final summary, is mainly a chronicle of incidents so mysterious, yet so personal and wonderfully consoling, that the yellowing typescript, taken from rough notes of each incident as it happened, has remained for lone years in a file. This file has been my most treasured possession and no eyes other than my own have scanned the precious notes that it holds.

However, I now strongly feel that I should share with other the strange phenomena that has been my experience – and phenomena is the only word that can best describe the wonderful happenings that befell me. I wish to share with others the indescribable joy and consolation that my unusual experiences brought to me, that in the sharing the reader can echo with me the words, "Oh grave, where is thy victory, oh death, where is thy sting".

Before I get down to detailing the strange events that befell me, I feel that I should first of all relate a very memorable incident which occurred on a cold, wintry day in early March 1960. It was Cannon Street, London, EC1, during the evening rush hour and I was wading my way homeward from work. I decided to buy an evening paper and so approached the News Vendor, a little woman huddled in a shawl against the keen wind. My hand was one of many in the queue proffering the price of the Evening News. As I awaited my turn I sighted a rather unusual paper for sale in the corner of her stall. It had an unusual heading, 'the Psychic News'. I can still recall the look of surprise and keen pleasure on the little woman's face as I requested this paper. I can still hear her words as I left with the paper, "You've got riches, my dear, you've got riches".

Yes, riches indeed were to be mine in the weeks and years that followed these prophetic words of the News Vendor, for in the phenomenal happenings that I experienced – which phenomena continued way into the late 1980's, which sadly has now all ceased. The reason for this cessation I cannot say, except that a legacy of comfort, the riches that the News Vendor spoke of so long ago, are indeed truly mine for the reality of all I heard, seen, even felt are as real to me today as I type this manuscript in the late 1990's as though they happened yesterday. The riches the News Vendor spoke of were not material riches, but the riches of spiritual enlightenment: I was to know the true meaning of the words of Jesus when he said; "and the truth shall set ye free", for , the astonishing, wonderful occurrences that surrounded me nightly, and as details in this book will relate, also in daylight as I sat at my office desk, from all this phenomena a great and wonderful truth has been revealed to me, that death is but an illusion, that it is but change only, change into a dimension or higher world of more evolved existence, where our loved ones await us, still caring, still loving, even crossing the barrier of death to comfort and console – and here once more I repeat my mother's wondrous, marvellous words to me, "here, beside you all the time".

I have related the episode of the Psychic News and the news vendor because I am convinced that the Cannon Street incident and the unusual prediction, "you've got riches....." was but the first link in a chain of psychic phenomena that was to follow, the leading part in the pattern of wondrous events that were to follow down through the years.

Chapter 1

It was March of the same year that I felt prompted to consult a well-known clairvoyant, Mrs Ivy Scott living in Clapham North, London. The evidence of survival that she gave to me in the three-quarter hour 'sitting' was undeniable and overwhelming, so much so that when I eventually left the little house in Clapham North on that memorable evening I felt I was walking on air, with excited joy, my heart was singing. For the first time in my life there was meaning and purpose in life where before there had been none, for, had it not just been revealed to me, been proved to me, that the brother I had mourned for as dead throughout the long sad years was not dead but very much alive. Bennie was living still. Living still, living still – these two words, those glorious words dominated my excited and happy mind that evening as I made my way homeward. Life continued, life went on, there was no death. Marvellous, marvellous thought. Where before, all through the long years following his passing, so great was my mental pain I could not bear even to hear his precious name spoken. Now it was a wonderful name to hear; now I can shout it at the heavens.

Regarding this memorable, wonderful night, this visit to Mrs Scott I must admit that despite the undeniable evidence given to me of my brother's continued existence, regardless of the indescribable joy and hope I carried home with me that evening, I nevertheless know only too well that, had it not been for the follow-up phenomenal happenings, my joyous convictions of this exciting night would have lost its strength and would likely have evaporated with the passage of time, for I'd still be clamouring in my analytical mind for PERSOANL proof. As a Roman Catholic child reared for nine long years in a convent in Ireland, I had been taught all the usual orthodox dogmatic religious teachings about hell-fire for the wicked and a heaven for the virtuous. Never was my young deep-thinking mind ever al all influenced by these teachings. It was not possible for me to be influenced because of my mind, childish as it was, rebelled against and always rejected such teachings. I just could not reconcile hell fire with a loving, merciful God. Young as I was, this teaching, dinned into us so much, just didn't make sense al all.

As I grew older, this critical, analytical side of my nature grew deeper; hence I never had any time for hearsay – the basis of so much mischief and harm to others. I always wanted and replied only on my own experiences, in personal proof. Such was the type of mind I had as a young child and which grew stronger into adulthood. Thus, as a child in the Irish Convent I know not the fear that these wrong teachings were meant to instil against possible wrong-doing, but neither did I know the consolation I was so badly in need of to assure the hidden grief I was harbouring for the father I was shedding nightly tears for, my father, Patrick, whom I had loved so much and had considered lost forever. He died when I was just seven years old, just prior to entering the convent as a boarder. My tears for the loss of him flowed on throughout most of my childhood, easing off somewhat as I entered my teens, for time gradually eases the pain, but, looking back now to my childhood I see it as a childhood bathed in grief and tears and it makes me feel sad. Still looking back, I recall the further terrible loss that was to be mine when in my early twenties my only brother, Bennie, hitherto mentioned, was taken from our household. As with my father, tuberculosis took him from us.

Here again in this further sorrow orthodox religious teaching failed to comfort. All the clergy had to offer by way of consolation were the insipid. Meaningless words, "your brother is with God". Such a lofty, vague statement did nothing to lessen my intense sorrow, a grief that, as already stated, pursued me throughout the long years but which ceased on the memorable night I visited Mrs Scott of Clapham North. God bless you, Mrs Scott: from the depths of my soul I thank you. That wonderful night was a night of great spiritual enlightenment, which revealed to me the stupendous truth that the loved one I had looked upon as dead was a whisper away in and around this earth in another dimension, that in reality there is no death and that, like the butterfly emerging from its chrysalis, the spirit moves on into continuous and higher life. Ah, that night in March 1960, what a wonderful night it was for me.

Chapter 2

I return now to that March night with all the outstanding evidence of survival that had been revealed to me, evidence which did not end as I left Mrs Scott's little house but which was about to multiply into phenomena that followed me home to my little bed-sit in London. On this particular night strange happenings began, phenomena which was only a beginning and which followed me throughout the long years ahead.

Shortly after I retired to bed I became aware of repeated soft knocking on my wardrobe door, light raps but distinct, and all the while there came from directly above my head a shower or sprinkling of what seemed like light hail or rain, disturbing my hair and tingling my face, It is important to mention here that this strange substance, this curious 'shower' pouring down on my head and face was not new to me as I experienced this same phenomena when, as a child at the convent, I knelt down by my bed to pray, my lonely, anxious young heart beseeching God to help my worried mother and cure my sick brother. Looking back now at that childish, trusting nightly routine, I am now convinced that there was a caring, unseen Presence with me during that time.

Now, so many years later, in my little room in London an unseen presence was with me once again. All sleet had abandoned me and I was keenly aware of this visitor in my room. I was excited, tense but unafraid for somehow I knew, coming directly after receiving the evidence of my brother's survival some hours before, I was convinced that it was none other that Bennie, drawn now to me in person from the unseen word that he now lived in through the link of contact with Mrs. Scott. I felt a great comfort and gradually my excited state diminished and I grew calm, staring, staring fascinated above my head at a greenish rod or beam of light from whence came the shower of what seemed and felt like light hail or rain, and tingling my cheeks. Gradually sleep overtook me and the night was uneventful.

And now I must draw the attention of the Reader to the remarkable substantiating further evidence regarding the mysterious substance which poured upon me, as related above. It came only many years later when I came across the self-same experience of a great Yogi, Paramahansa Yoganda, in which he related his own phenomenal experience. And here I quote his written words, as follows:-

"My room was dimly lit by two shaded lamps. Lifting my gaze, I noticed that the ceiling was dotted with small mustard-coloured lights, scintillating and quivering with a radium-like lustre. *Myriads of penciled rays, like sheets of rain, gathered into a transparent shaft and poured silently upon me. At once my physical body lost its grossness and became metamorphosed (change of form) into astral texture. I felt a floating sensation as, barely touching the bed, my weightless body shifted slightly and alternatively to left and right".

This was the amazing quote that my eyes fell upon so many years later, confirming my own phenomenal experience. Note the words he uses which correspond with the description of the substance which I scribbled in my rough notes early each morning when I awoke. These notes I scribbled down each day or early morning as it was so important for each nightly incident to be kept fresh in my memory (and may I say here that it is from these long, rough scribbled notes that this manuscript is formed, for you, dear reader, to share).

From the great Yogi's quote I have underlined the words he uses as they are almost exactly to mine. For instance, "Sheets of rain", "transparent shaft" (my description, 'rod or bean', pencilled rays, pouring upon me'). There's no denying that this great man's experience regarding the mysterious rays, an experience of so many years before, was confirmation of my own, verification which excited and delighted me.

The peculiar happenings of this march night, the pouring substance from above my head, the rapping, this was but a forerunner to future phenomena that I was to witness in the weeks and throughout the long years that followed, when I gradually began to accept as natural the existence of an intervening world and the living presence of loved ones once considered lost forever. As the Newsvendor had foretold, riches indeed became mine.

Monday Night, 11th April – Easter week.

It was one month later my visit to Mrs Scott and during this month my little back bedroom in Streatham was a hive of unseen phenomenal activity, which I had so grown used to that the world when I entered was completely shut our and I basked in the comfort that the unseen presence nightly brought me. On this particular night I retired to bed around

10.30pm. When I switched off the light I noticed that the peculiar greenish-blue rays which had been appearing in my room were even more pronounced, and indeed the room was literally lit up with these rays. I lay in the darkness staring at this strange happening and trying to fathom out the cause, all thought of sleep gone. I arose and looked out the window but the little backyard was so normal, in its usual darkness. No solution to the rays was found there. There was no moon visible, no clue to the strange puzzle of the rays going back and forth across the ceiling in the little room. All was silent, except for an occasional tap on the wardrobe door. Back into bed I went, where I lay fascinated and with an unusual expectation as I gazed at the wide rays which moved to and fro across the ceiling. Directly above my head the usual misty rod or beam of light lingered, appearing and disappearing, whilst from it there poured down upon my face the tingling substance that I had grown used to, but this particular night the beam was stronger than was usual and the substance more heavy. There was no mistaking the fact that this sprinkling or shower skin to the feel of hail or rain was without doubt coming from the beam of misty light above my head. I must mention here that on through the years until the late 1980's this strange substance continued to fall upon me nightly and from this nightly shower I derived the utmost comfort, as it intimated that loving unseen loved ones were with me. When this particular phenomenon ceased as the 1980's passed away, I felt bereft of the consolation I had revelled in.

Reverting back to this night, all drowsiness had left me as I gazed at the sprinkling beam of light above me and in particular at the walls of the little room which had completely disappeared into a mist of the same bluish-green hue as the rod of light above me. I was somewhat tense but not frightened and full of expectation as I was aware that something momentous was about to happen. I tried to pierce the mist in the room but in vain, it was growing thicker. Gradually, sleep started to overcome me, then, all drowsiness went as I was made fully alert by the distinct sound of a step in the centre of the room, near the dressing table. I tensed into full wakefulness, keenly alert once more. I lay thus for a while and all became quiet, no further sound in the little room. I become relaxed and sleepy once more. As I was drifting off I was aroused to full wakefulness by the very distinct sound of the step once again, but this time it was not by my dressing table but close beside me, by me bedside. I grew very tense, but strangely all tension went the sudden caressing, a light caressing of my hair. This disturbance over my hair was a further phenomenon, as it had been happening nightly over many weeks as I was drifting off to sleep. I had grown used to it and it brought me a great measure of comfort.

This time, however, the caressing did not lift and I did not drift off to sleep. It continued with more pressure, as if a tangible something were on my head. The pressure increased until I felt myself enveloped in darkness with a feeling of being crushed, accompanied by a distinct cold breeze. I felt frightened as I was aware something very unusual was about to take place. I knew not what, so I was naturally very tense. Strangely then I began to mentally communicate, not with words, I didn't seem to need words. I became aware of myself saying, mentally, "you must go back, you must go back". I knew I was not alone, that there was a definite unseen presence with me. It was at this crucial and rather frightening point that it happened. All tension left me as, wonder of wonders, I felt a hand in mine beneath the bedclothes, a man's hand, with long, slim, warm and very alive fingers, a hand which drew all tension from me. I felt completely relaxed; I knew a comfort I had never before known. Then, just as though someone had whispered to me, there came the certain knowledge that the hand that was holding mine was the precious hand of Bennie, who had left this earth so long ago in October 1945. As this conviction came to me I lost all fear and ceased struggling, as I had been struggling to escape from the pressure and the darkness. Immediately I ceased 'fighting' and relaxed, the pressure and darkness miraculously lifted and so clearly now I saw a face, a well-loved face, a once familiar face which time had dimmed the memory of.

Without any doubt, there before me was the dear face of Bennie, my brother. It was there in all its clarity, in its every detail. Words cannot describe the amazement and joy I felt, the thrilling excitement and sense of happiness that enveloped my whole being. What impressed me most was the radiant peace of his countenance, the memory of which has remained with me ever since. His vividly blue eyes, which time had dimmed the memory of, there were before my wondering gaze, serene and smiling. I would mention here that in the long, sad years since his passing there had been one favourite and haunting old tune, namely, "two eyes of blue came smiling through". This tune, whenever I heard it had brought me so much pain in the memory of his vivid blue eyes. However, here they were, smiling at me once again. Every detail of his dear countenance was there before me. I noted the long, delicate nose, the lovely impressive difference. His face was no longer the face of an immature youth. It was the countenance of a mature man, a face filled out, no longer thin, the expression one of serenity and wisdom, of complete peace. His hair in particular I noticed, parted on the right side as I had known it and the same light brown colour. I recall clearly how I mentally communicated with him, by saying excitedly, not really as a question by as a confirming statement, "Bennie, is it really you?" I had no sense of doubt. It was just a joyful statement. I knew it was he, for wasn't he there before me in all his reality. I do not recall his making a reply but I feel maybe his smile was his acquiescence, his way of agreeing, 'here I am'. We conversed, not in words, as hitherto said, but mentally. The conversation seemed to be one-sided, for when he had gone I could only recall my own excited words and little of his. The curious part of this phenomenon was the fact that there was no verbal communication but a mental one. I was talking with my mind – words seemed to be flowing from my mind to his, and vice versa – words were not necessary.

I suppose one could call this experience 'telepathy', which only in later years became an accepted phenomenon in society. One question I clearly recall putting to my brother was a reference to a youthful friend of his, by querying, "You remember Harry Bailie, Bennie?" I had not thought of this person in years, yet his name came foremost in my mind as I ask the question. How vividly do I recall his smile of assent? Words were not necessary for I seemed to read his mind. Then, I had the feeling that someone else prompted me to say, "you must go back now, Bennie, you must go back". As I mentally advised him to do this he started to recede away from me, but then slowly came back, smiling as before. I then put another question to him, "What do you do now, Benie?" So vividly do I recall his strange reply, just two words, 'I divide". Divide what, Bennie, I asked. His answer, even stranger than before, "units of electrical capacity". I recall his brief smile of hesitation as he began to speak these curious words, accompanied by a smile that seemed to say, "You wouldn't understand", which of course I did not, nor to this day. If this be all a dream, I thought later, then from whence these mystifying words came and what did they mean. One doesn't dream up such words, words which have greatly puzzled me all through these years. Then, suddenly as before, I had the urge to say to him, "You must go back now, Bennie, you must go back". Once again he began to recede from me, smiling as he went, only to return once more. Again we conversed, but of this conversation I later retained no memory, except to recall saying, for the third time, as if I were prompted by some other invisible presence to do so, "you must go back now, Bennie, you must go back", this time adding, "but you'll come back again, won't you?"

"Of course I will", he smilingly replied as he slowly faded from me, disappearing from, my sight. No longer was he there, in my world. He had gone. I then noticed that my little back-room, where all this tremendous happening had taken place, was now back to normal. Gone were the moving rays from the ceiling, the green fog or mist from the walls, which were now visible again. I sat up in bed, my being thrilled with the excitement and joy of the wondrous phenomena I had been so privileged to witness. I felt like shouting aloud to the sleeping world, "my brother is not dead – he's alive for I've just seen and talked to him".

I recall looking with purpose at the clock, as I wished the time of these precious moments to always remain with me, which indeed thy have. The hands of the little clock, as I stated was 2.35am. His last words, his promise to me to return, "of course I will", will be forever with me. I have not seen him since, but I have no doubt at all that he is with me now and then, though I cannot see him. I can only consider that his so special visit, his making himself visible to me, was a very unusual and doubtless difficult effort on his part, and on the part of those invisible presences I had sensed were with him in my little room. I would mention here that as he was finally receding from me, I had the urge to say to him, "Give my love to my father and all".

These words came from a keen sense that the unseen presence that I was aware of accompanied my brother was my other most dearly loved ones whom I had shed such bitter tears for during my 16 years long childhood reign in the convent, my dear father.

Tuesday Night – April 12th

If last night's joyous, phenomenal event was but a dream, then this following night brought a continuation of that dream, but to a lesser extent. I retired to bed around 11.30pm. My kind and very caring little landlady, Delia, had retired much earlier and thus the little house in Streatham was very quiet and still, as on the previous night. As I settled down to try and sleep I noticed that the mysterious, wide, greenish-blue base-like rays of the night before were once more gathering in the ceiling on my room. I became even more fascinated as I noticed the walls gradually beginning to fade behind a bluish mist, as on the previous night. Now and then I heard movement around the room. I was unafraid and full of expectation of my brother's return.. This was not to be, however. As I lay in excited anticipation, all thought of sleep now gone. As I surveyed the moving rays, the misty walls, looking directly then above my head there once more was the distinct greenish-blue 'rod' or 'beam' of light. As I lay studying this curious beam, there suddenly came ploy down upon my face the tingling shower or hail-like substance that had descended upon me the previous night. Each time I gazed upwards at the beam or rod of light, a shower of a tingling substance would descend upon me. I was fascinated by this and continued to gaze upwards trying to fathom the strange phenomena. Becoming drowsy, sleep was beginning to overtake me when I was brought to full conscious alertness by a distinct tap on my little bedside table. I heard more movement in various parts of the room. I was conscience of a presence in the room, close by my bed. I was slightly tense in expectation but not al all frightened, for I was fully aware that the presence beside me was caring, loving, and protective. I was hoping it was Bennie once again. However, nothing unusual happened. I felt keen disappointment, and then sleep gradually overtook me.

Wednesday Morning, April 13th – During Office Hours

Now during my lunchtime in my job as a typist in the Government here at Whitehall, I am taking the opportunity to record in type the precious details of all that has mysteriously occurred in my little room since the beginning of the Easter Week, as an unforgettable memoir for the years ahead as human memory can be frail, and, however impressive the experience, can with the passing of time grow less vivid and even fade completely. So, as I sit here on a Wednesday morning at my desk in Whitehall, I seem to be re-born. I am filled with a happiness I'd never known before, for, hadn't the brother I had mourned for visited me and proved to me that hw still lived. That being so, life itself took on a new, glorious meaning, for new I realized that in all of God's creation there was no death, all was eternal, CHANGE only. Life now MADE SENSE. It was a glorious world outside my window. Hope reigned.

And so, dear reader, here now as I type the details of Easter Week's phenomena, more wondrous proof was to follow. The light, the mist in my room, the vision of my brother, was not a wonderful fantasy of dream. It is here with me now in the light of day even as I type, for the unfathomable tingling shower of the hail-like substance that kept pouring down on my face in my little room is falling on me now, tingling my face as before, but now this substance is visible to my eyes as it drops like stardust on a Christmas tree onto the paper on my desk. For me, no better proof of the reality of the preceding phenomena could there be than this wonderful repetition here in the broad light of day. This morning I have been given incontrovertible evidence of the survival of my brother whom I had considered gone forever. Now I can fully appreciate the meaning of the biblical words, "Oh grave, where is thy victory, oh death, where is thy sting?"

Onward march the years and tragedy strikes our family once again. The year 1965 shows my mother losing hold on life. A cancerous tumour has developed In her chest, its daily growth ominously telling us that her days are numbered. My two sisters and I were filled with a deep anxiety and distress at the signs that we were about to lose her, for she was the sun of our lives, the loving centre of our little family. We were filled with a terrible dread that in the going from this world she would suffer much, as the swelling just below her neck had grown so large we assumed that it would either choke her or it would burst and she would bleed to death. The thought of perhaps having to witness this fate happening to one we loved so dearly was almost impossible to bear. My mother was severely crippled with arthritis in her legs and hip and was mostly confined to her chair – the little armchair that even to this day I still possess and shall always cherish. She could walk only with great difficulty. When she attempted to do so she suffered not only physical pain but great frustration and depression of mind, such terrible frustration making her at times irritable, as she had been such an active person all her life. Our deep concern for her, the awful waiting for the ultimate catastrophe, how it would come about, the anxious question in all our minds, "would she suffer much?" left my sisters and myself suffering from insomnia and keyed up with tension.

It was in this state of turmoil and distress that I retired to bed one night in March this sad year. I had taken a sleeping pill in an endeavour to combat my insomnia and make me sleep. The pill had the desired effect and I fell into a deep sleep. Around 5am I awoke and surprisingly found myself gazing into a somewhat familiar face, a stern and unsmiling face, a countenance I had not been thinking of nor had reason to be thinking of, even though the owner of the face was a person for whom I held the utmost respect and admiration for had he not been the only Pontiff to visit the prisons on his first official duty. His first thought when he took over his very high office was to do as Jesus urged for hadn't He advised, "leave the ninety-nine and go seek the sheep that is lost". Yes, here before me in my little room was that same dear man, Pope John 23rd, his face very stern, his finger pointing at me as he advised, "you must be patient, you must be patient, you must be patient".

Three times he repeated these words and then disappeared from my view. Regarding his pointing finger, it was years later that I came upon a large painting of him with pointing finger, which picture I immediately purchased and which hangs upon my bedroom wall today, a very cherished reminder of his early morning visit, and advice, many years before. I lay wide awake and pondered on the vision I had seen. I instinctively knew he was chiding me for letting the sad situation regarding my mother get on top of me. I felt he was urging me to have courage and not to succumb to the crisis that had hit our little household. I also felt greatly comforted, for I somehow knew that he was aware of the distress we all within our little family were undergoing. I was aware he was telling me to be calm, that ultimately our dear mother would be alright, whatever the outcome of her illness. As I lay and pondered over his visit, I felt wonderfully consoled and the enlightening thought occurred to m, "if Pope John is ALIVE, so eventually when mother passed she too would still live". Round and round in my head came the reassuring conviction, "Pope John is alive, there is no death, no need for despair". Dear, dear Pope John, there is a deep well of eternal thanks within my soul for the great consolation you give me on that wonderful morning so many years ago. Mother passed away peacefully on the 8th September 1965. What we had anticipated in our terrible anxiety did not happen. She died in her sleep, without pain. Pope John had been right, all was indeed well in the end.

Why did Pope John 23rd visit me, I often asked myself throughout the years that followed, for , though I firmly believed in prayer, in communication with any unseen higher power and always from early childhood talked to the unseen power privately, I had no interest in Church dogma or church going? Yet this great spiritual man visited little me from beyond the grave. It was a puzzle so, until one day I found what I now consider to be the answer, to be the link that brought him to my little room on that morning long ago. Many years later I came upon a little booklet on his life, which little book I still cherish, like his picture, today. Upon reading this little book I cam upon a most revealing and significant fact, that fact that Pope John's mother had a very old-fashioned name, that of Mary Ann, the self same precious name as my own dear mother. This revelation made me realise that he loved his mother just as dearly as I loved mine. The very old-fashioned name, Mary Ann, was the key, the golden link, which drew him back to the sad world he had left, in full understanding of the anxiety and sense of coming loss that our little family were undergoing. Dear Pope John 23rd, no greater Pope of the Vatican has there been, a man of great love and a great loss to the world, even, as before stated, visiting the prisons, which to my recollection (and here I may be wrong), no Pontiff has ever done before or since. I was indeed privileged.

But this great spiritual man, Pope John, did not forget me when he faded from my sight on that amazing night, for he returned, and I feel he returned to prove to me that his visit on that morning had indeed really happened. He had not quite said 'goodbye'. Two years after my mother's passing, as I lay in my bed in my lonely London Bed-sitter, there he was before me once more. As I opened my sleepy eyes in the early morning hours he was before me once more in full reality. This time, however, there was a difference. This time he was smiling at me and not stern and he was gone. I have not seen him since. Dear, dear Pope John, how can I ever thank you!

Chapter 3

I have so many phenomenons still to relate regarding the passing of my mother. In January 1966, just a few short months after she left her little family, the love that was stronger than death brought her back to comfort us. She came to console her family through many, many visits to me. The dates and details of which I now relate:

1st January 1966
In the early hours of this morning I slowly awakened from sleep to find myself gazing for about a full twenty seconds into a pair of familiar eyes, the eyes of my mother. But, what different eyes! They were bright, calm, serene and wise, completely devoid of their old unhappy and tired look that I had known throughout her declining years and during her illness. They were young eyes, happy eyes. Then they were gone, conveying to me a happiness and blissful peace, the memory which thrilled me all through the remaining hours.

3rd January 1966
Just two nights later she came again. What blissful phenomena, the memory of which still thrills my being. I awoke on this night with the very definite feel of a soft, small hand in mine, beneath the bedclothes. At this point I was drowsy, but becoming more awake and alert there was no mistaking the reality of the feeling of the little hand that held mine. I had a wonderful awareness of a great contentment and peace and had no inclination even to stir. I had a great feeling of complete security as I pressed the little hand underneath the bedclothes in joyful response and welcome. As I held her hand I recalled her precious

wedding ring of my mother. Then I recalled her so precious wedding ring which was on a chain around my neck. I fumbled and found the ring, pressing it into the little hand which held mine, holding the hand tight, tight, as I contentedly drifted off into a deep sleep. I would mention here that so great was the sense of security and contentment I felt, so utterly convinced of my mother's presence, I had no sense of curiosity, no wish to do anything by cling, like a small child, to the precious hand within my own and so back into sleep.

12th January 1966

In the early hours of this morning I was awakened by someone gently lifting the bedclothes off my shoulders. As on other occasions, I was drowsy but alert to the fact that there was an arm around my shoulders and that there was a presence gently bending over me. I was not nervous but very much at ease for I was deeply aware that my mother was with me once more. Unlike her last visit, I had the urge to turn around to see her fully. I turned over on my right side and, there she was in full reality, my mother who had just left this world but a few short months before. There she was before my gaze, vital, alive, so happy, so young, young as I knew her in childhood. She looked about thirty years old or less. I was particularly impressed with her new-found youth. I was struck by her radiance, her look of peaceful happiness and I was aware of her excited sense of delight at being with me. Gone was the old care-worn look. I could feel the reality of her arms around me, warm, loving, familiar arms. Then the dear voice that I knew so well clearly said, with an excitement that lies in a great discovery, "Look, I can walk – I can even run – and I can work like I used to". She then proceeded to move her right arm, with a motion with that I then took to be baking bread. Three times she moved her right arm in this motion. Suddenly, and beyond explanation, I was no longer in my bed but walking down a street with her, a street like any normal street in this world, a street full of shops and shoppers, normal people going about their normal business, some carrying shopping bags dressed in familiar attire. As I walked by my mother's side I was aware that my mother was youthful, that she was tall and straight, not bent and old. She was her busy, active self as in days gone by. I was so happy, so contented, walking by her side, and full of wonder in the certain awareness that I was no longer on the earth but in another dimension, another world, a world to which I knew I did not yet belong. I stared into the face of one little woman passing by, carrying a shopping bag; I looked closely at her face to speak to her but she just looked through me; she could not see me. Yes indeed, though I walked happily by my mother's side, I knew I did not belong in this new world of hers. With my mother we entered a small grocer's shop where we queued with other women waiting to be served by a lady behind a counter. The grocer's shop was a familiar one, one from the past, not a supermarket as in the world I had left behind in sleep. My mother spoke to me saying, "I must get some currants!" As she uttered these words the strange yet so familiar scene vanished and I was aware of being back again in my bed in my London bed-sitter, back in the world I had left. I lay for a long time, thrilled and excited by the wondrous reality of the scene I had partaken of. I was conscious of my mother's presence still with me. Then, doubts came. Was it all but a dream? As this thought entered my excited my mind, from above my head came a distinct splash of the **hail-like substance that I had grown to know so well, splash down upon my eyes, completely dispersing all my doubts. No indeed, it had not been just a dream. I had been in the company of my mother in her new world.

**The reoccurrence of this 'splashing' phenomenon from above my head had been a nightly occurrence since I saw my brother, Bennie, on that memorable night of Easter Week in 1960.

January 13th 1966
On this night I awakened, felt thirsty and got out of bed for some water. On getting back into bed I lay thinking, thinking, and quiet unable to get back to sleep again. Then once again, as on the previous night, there came an arm around my shoulders, this time accompanied by a distinct cold breeze. As on the night of the 12th January I was not al all apprehensive. My only desire was to see my mother again, for I was in no doubt but that she was with me once more. As before, I turned from lying on my side hoping to see her but saw no one. Clearly then I heard my name called in my mother's unmistakable tone, the way she alone used to say it, "Josà", the accent being strongly on the à. I could feel her presence but could not see her. I kept repeating, "Mammie, where are you". I heard very distinct whispering replies but the sounds seemed far away and thus I could not make out what she was saying. The whispering continued, then receded until all ceased.

30th January 1966
On this night, just a loud, clearly whispered "Josà", so loud in fact that it startled me wide awake in the early hours – just the one call of my name in my mother's voice, but oh, how welcome the sound.

31st January 1966

This particular night was indeed one to be remembered, as it confirmed all the phenomena of the previous nights. During my sleep I felt a continuous tickling under my chin, a very persistent tickling which finally awoke me. On awakening I immediately became aware that I was unusually hot. I felt for the switch of my electric under-blanket and realised that I had not turned it off, which I usually did before sleeping. I turned the switch off and lay pondering. In my mind come the thought, "someone has been trying to waken me as I am in danger from the blanket". Upon this thought entering my mind I recalled my mother's teasing habit of tickling me in the self-same way, underneath my chin. As I lay marvelling at this revelation I became aware of a pressure bearing down on my bed, and then, there it was again, the little hand in mine, as before. This time, however, not only did I feel a soft, small hand, but I also felt a warm, soft arm. I was drowsy and had no curiosity whatever for there was nothing to be curious about, because I was fully aware that my dear mother was with me again. I was utterly contact just to hold onto the hand and drift back into sleep. In my drowsy state I remembered her wedding ring, which was, as always, on a chain around my neck. Sleepily I fumbled for it, and then having found it I pressed it tightly into her small palm. Drowsily I lay for awhile, holding her hand with the ring within its palm, close, close. Then clearly I recall lifting the little hand that enclosed her wedding ring to my lips and kissing it. I was aware of a great feeling of security, peace and contentment. All this while I was in a very drowsy state but not asleep, fully aware of my mother's presence. The, stranger indeed than fiction, the tiny hand in mine changed and I became aware that I was now holding a lard hand, a man's hand. I then felt an arm, a strong, brawny man's arm. This hand I also sleepily rose to my lips and kissed, repeating with my mind the words, "you are so good, you are so good". I recall the deep feeling of gratitude I felt as I repeated these words, as I was aware that the owner of this hand had brought my mother to me. As I lay holding this hand I drifted into a deep sleep.

Chapter 4

And now, dear reader, before I leave the year 1966, this year of so much consolation and joy, I would like to return to the night of January 12th when my mother excitedly and joyously told me, "Look, I can walk – I can even run – and I can work like I used to". So vividly do I recall how these statements were made, in three excited bursts of a joyful discovery? The motion she made going round and round three times with her right arm, demonstrating the work she was portraying, had never really satisfied my then assumption that she was symbolising the action of baking bread. In the back of my mind I had always felt that the motion portrayed something else. Then, out of the blue, a few months later, the full and true realisation burst upon my mind. The motion she had been portraying was that of the action of ironing. This revelation made me feel stupid and ashamed. Why, oh why, didn't I realise the truth before. You see, for thirty long arduous years my mother had worked in the laundry two miles outside the town as an ironer, work that she had proudly and conscientiously carried out and loved. Now she could work again "like she used to". This was the happy message she had been trying to convey to me. The important fact of my mother working as an ironer was completely forgotten by me, due to the fact that she had ceased this work many years before owing to severe arthritis in her hip. She was no longer able to make the long 2 mile walk to the laundry. In all those long years, come hail, come shine, I don't think she even missed a day. I can still hear her proudly say during those years, "I've never been a day off sick in my life – God fits the back for the burden". The burden she referred to was the responsibility of rearing four young children when my father died at the young age of 41 from tuberculosis. My dear hard-working mother. Nothing stopped her during those thirty long years from reaching her place of work as an ironer, and nothing stopped her on this wonderful night of 12th January in coming back to console me, to give me the UKTIMATE PROOF that she still lived.

Chapter 5
1967

If the year 1966 is a memorable one for me, so also is this year of 1967. Scarcely a night went by without my mother making me aware of her presence. There was scarcely a night or early morning that she did not call my name, usually when just drifting into sleep, when her familiar voice calling "Josephine", occasionally "Josà", would startle me awake. In the early morning, when it was time to arise for work, she would awaken me. But there were other voices, voices which I did not recognise. There was the voice of the little lady who came so often, just to say the one word 'hello' in a gentle, drawling tone. I always visualised this lady as a small, timid, gentle, elderly lady, for her tone was just that, timid and gentle. This little lady came every now and then throughout the years, but recently has ceased to come. The last time she made her presence known was in 12982. I often wonder about her, as to whom she may be. Then there was the male voice which just said, so loud and clear, the one word, 'goodnight'. This was a greeting I received when I had just settled into bed and was very wide awake. This was a cultured, educated tone. I wondered too about him. He never returned. Oh, how lonely I felt when all these voices ceased. This year of 1967 was a most impressive year indeed. It was a year when the veil between two worlds was very thin indeed, a year in which I was continually reminded that I was not alone, that my loved ones surrounded me nightly. Such was the closeness of my loved ones, such was my awareness of the reality of their presence within my little room, that the one and only conclusion I could come to was that the world to which we pass at death interpenetrates this physical world in which we all live. Every thing shouted aloud this fact to me. The reality of the voices, the gentle touches on my hair, the warm breath on my face, all this phenomena told me of the presence of loved ones that had preceded me from this world. Confirming this conviction of mine, this belief that the next world interpenetrated this one, was a firm assurance of this when in reply to a question I put to my mother, :mother, this is wonderful - where have you been?", her significant answer was, "here beside you, all the time".

So real had my nightly visitors become that I looked forward with much anticipation to going to bed each night. On the odd nights when they did not come – and odd nights there were – I felt forlorn and disappointed, like a child when its mother fails to come to say 'goodnight'. One very familiar and mysterious phenomenon was the blowing of a warm breath in my face each morning to across me from sleep in time to get up for work. As I have already told you, dear reader, insomnia was my bed-fellow and so I had to take a nightly sleeping pill. This enforced habit of mine resulted in difficulty coming out of sleep in good time for work. It was so obvious from this blowing in my face each morning that the loved ones who surrounded me were aware of this problem and their help in this respect clearly showed their care for my well-being. Their method of arousal was to continuously blow a warm breath upon my face until I gradually awoke from my comatose type sleep. As the warm breath fanned my face, occasionally I would slip back into sleep but the breath perseveringly continued until I was finally fully awake.

Before I leave the year 1967 I should like to relate just another example of the devotion and care my unseen loved one bestowed upon me. It was a day when I struggled through work at the office with a nagging pain in my left side. Hence, upon retiring to bed that night I was distressed and exhausted and shed bitter tears. After much tossing and inability to sleep I eventually did sleep but was awakened later with the caressing over my hair that I had grown so familiar with. As this particular touching of my hair went on, my mother's clear voice said: "she's alright now". The caressing continued until, much comforted, I fell asleep again. As these words of my mother, "she's alright now", reached my ears, I was aware that she was speaking to other unseen presences with her. Later on in that year I had a return of this pain and was subsequently operated upon for gall stones at St. Bartholomew's hospital, London.

Chapter 6
January 1968

It was during the above month that I was privileged indeed, privileged to see the animals I had loves and considered lost forever. I had a vision that revealed to me a very special truth, the wonderful truth that animals also survive the grave. I now gladly share in these pages my wonderful, never to be forgotten vision with animal lovers everywhere.

On this particular and very special night I found myself in the sleep state in a large green field. I was fully aware that the scene I found myself a part of was not of the earth I left behind in sleep. I was fully aware that I was in another world, for how could it be otherwise, it was so wonderfully different. Awe-struck I gazed at the beauty of my surroundings. No grass of the world I had left could compete with the vivid green of the hill top upon which I now stood, no sun of the world I knew was as radiant as this, a radiance that shone with glare. All I can say is that a spiritual sun shone over all bathing the scene in a beauty I had never known. But the best was yet to come, for there across the green landscape looking towards me with anticipation and recognition was an unforgettable sight, a sight which will reign within my heart forever. There facing me, standing on the right of my mother, young, serene and smiling as she pointed at her feet to introduce me the beloved pets of days gone by. There he was, my darling Prince, the black and white mongrel dog which I had loved so much, the mongrel which mother had taken in as a starving stray and who lived with our family for 16 years: there beside him was Blackie, my spaniel dog, whom we all had loved and lost and so sadly missed. I stared in delight and disbelief tat these two old and very dear friends of mine: the excitement and love that showed in their eyes matched the great live that poured out of my soul for them. Recognition was the keynote. It was aglow in their eyes – they knew me, they remembered me after all the long sad years of parting. But, how different they looked: health just shone from their coats that had grown so dull when I knew them. They too shared in the spiritual glow that dominated the whole scene. But, more joy was to come. There, standing on the left of the joyous company was my dear brother, Bennie, smiling a message across at me, a message which clearly said, as he pointed at the animals, the happy dogs, and, believe it or not, my dear long-lost pussy-cats, there you are, his introduction clearly said, "there is no death – for anyone".

My pussycats, they too knew me, the recognition in their eyes was unmistakable, and, despite all the years between, I knew each individual one of them. May God bless you, my dear mother and brother for the great joy you brought me this night? As I stared in amazement at the scene, Prince darted towards me and left the group, heading straight for my welcoming arms, where upon reaching me he lay still with contentment as he nestled against my left shoulder. Without further movement he lay and I had the feeling he could have nestled there forever. As I held him, I saw also dear Shot, another long-lost friend waiting beside Blackie the mongrel, both on the alert and ready to spring towards my arms. Then, alas, the glorious vision was to end. All the loved ones disappeared as I awoke in my little London bed-sitter, back to the world I had left. I lay awake, all further sleep gone as I revelled in the wonder of what I had witnessed. To all animal lovers the message I impart to you is so clear. All life is indestructible and love is the key that opens the door to glorious reunion. I say to al who mourn their animal companions, | dry your tears". Animals too survive – despite the wrong dogmatic teaching that animals have 'no souls'. I say again, all life is indestructible and this fact was brought home to me by my loved ones. If I saw my animal friends – and I did – so too, will all ye who mourn your pets. They too await your coming and you shall hug them once more.

And so I move to February of this same year, for here within my faded notes I come to what I have entitled, "my starry vision". This particular and very strange vision I gave this title as a starry vision, for indeed, that was what it was. It was an event so startling, so mysterious, that it is one of my most vivid memories, for, unlike my sleep-state visions, this phenomenon happened when I was wide awake and sleep was beyond me. As I mentioned earlier in this book, I suffered almost daily with migraines and this particular day in February was far from being an exception. I was completely exhausted at the end of the day and retired to bed around 9.30 pm. My only desire was to seek solace in sleep. However, sleep evaded me and I tossed restlessly through the long hours. Eventually I gave up my efforts to sleep and lay on my back, gazing into the darkness, my mind disturbed and worried as to how I was able to arise in time for work. As I lay thus, I became aware of myriad pin-points of starry lights vibrating within my little room. I lay fascinated, all thought of work gone form my mind. As I stared in amazement, the tiny pin-points of light continued to vibrate. Round and round, faster and faster, larger and larger they grew, coming closer and closer to me until the shone of my little room became like the starry heavens that one sees from the vantage point of a planetarium. Then, I say it now, sadly the speed of the vibrating lights frightened my; I felt something stupendous was about to happen and the fear of the unknown caused my to move my finger to the switch of my bedside lamp and I turned on the electric light. Everything was normal, for many minutes I lay thus, too scared to turn the light off again. Eventually I did so. The 'starry vision' had gone, never again to return. Looking back on this night, how I do regret having turned on the light. I feel sure that, had I not done so, something momentous but spiritual and good for me would have occurred, some spiritual revelation that was meant to comfort me, considering that I was in much need of comfort. Long have I wished for a repetition of the phenomena of this 'starry vision' but it was not to be. I would gladly welcome the experience again, for in the knowledge and clearer understanding that I have since gained, I would have no apprehension and the phenomena would reveal its meaning and purpose to me.

Chapter 7

And now I move on in this year to Easter. I had felt lonely and forlorn all over the holiday, partly because my sister, Sheila, who had been working in London with me, had returned home to Ireland and partly because I had received unexpected and very brief notice to quit my bed-sitter which I had occupied for over a year and in which I was settled and contented. Hence, anxious to get settled, I left my accommodation on the Easter Saturday to search for other accommodation, which resulted in my finding another bed-sitter. I was exhausted from moving my luggage to the new accommodation and could not afford a taxi for the two runs required. Thus, when I had settled into my new 'digs' at the end of this Easter weekend, I felt worn-out, dejected and very homesick. I still felt like this when I retired to bed on Easter Monday night. However, after have taken a sleeping pill I eventually slept, only to waken about 3.00am. Then the distressing events of the weekend crowded in on my mind, leaving me upset and restless. It was some considerable time before I drifted back into sleep again. Later I awoke to full wakefulness, only to realise I was lying on my back, a position in sleep which was unusual for me. As I lay thus, I gradually became aware of a hand lying across my forehead. I thought this rather peculiar, for somehow, sleepy as I was, I had a strong feeling that the hand on my forehead was not my own hand. As this thought entered my mind I became aware of my own hands beneath the bedclothes. As I lay pondering on this enigma I did not feel at all nervous but was filled with a curious sense of wellbeing, excitement and anticipation. I waited for the hand on my forehead to lift but it still remained gently upon my forehead. The though then came, "I wonder if it's my mother's hand – I must find out". With complete confidence and trust I moved my right hand from beneath the bedclothes, stretched upwards towards my forehead and touched, marvel of marvels, a worm and very much alive hand. The strange hand lay completely still as my own small hand explored it, feeling a skin of unusual texture, fine, silky, human and warm to my touch. I had felt hands on my forehead before, twice a small lady's hand, and once the strong, large hand of a man, but these earlier experiences only lasted about 12 seconds or so, the hand lifting almost as soon as I became aware of it. This particular hand, however, had now been on my forehead about over a full minute or so as I caressed and pondered on it, and how long it had lain upon my forehead previous to my awakening was the big question.

I realised as my fingers explored it that this hand was again a large, masculine hand. I then had a sudden urge to kiss it and was filled with a deep surge of emotional gratitude. I instinctively knew that the owner of this hand was a loving, caring person, come specially to comfort me in my depressed state. I ceased to caress the hand and then, as though its owner had anticipated my wish, I was permitted to raise it to my lips, when I gently kissed it with a feeling of reverence and love. The hand was then withdrawn and I drifted contentedly into a restful sleep. That was so remarkable about this phenomena was the fact that I had no desire to see beyond the hand, no curiosity to see its owner. I was just happily secure in the knowledge that someone most caring and good was with me, and the felling I had as the hand withdrew was one of utter confidence and complete trust.

Chapter 8

And now I move two years further on, to 1969/70. During these two years I was left in no doubt that my unseen loved ones, my nightly visitors, were still with me, caring for me. Nightly, almost without exception, and even some times on awakening in the mornings, my Christian name was clearly called. Living alone in London, where my world consisted mainly of my lonely little bed-sitter and my place of work in the City, it was rarely, if ever, that I heard my Christian name. Hence it was more than just consolation I received when my name, 'Josà', sometimes 'Josephine' was called each night. It was sheer joy and I no longer felt the awful feeling of loneliness that life in London brings.

The call of my name by my loved ones was a precious reminder that I was not just a mere number within the vast teeming millions of humanity that traversed the Capital. The love that came with the call of my name vanished that dreadful image.

It was nearing the end of 1970 when I had one of my happiest dreams, a dream so vivid, so real and so lovely that I must relate it to you. In the sleep state I found myself 'floating' up a steep embankment. Notice I state 'floating' and not walking. I was literally sailing up the little green hill. The main feeling I had was that I was in another world where I just did not really belong. I say 'lovely' as I was keenly alert to the beautiful scene that I was now a part of, as I 'floated' up for the vivid green of the grass was the same unusual green of the hilltop on which my mother and brother brought my animal friends to me, as hitherto related. Now I was back again in that same beautiful new world. As for the colours of the flowers that bedecked the embankment on which I stood, words just fail to describe their deep radiance; no colours on earth could surpass their hue. The sweetness of their fragrance was almost over-powering. As I reached the top of the embankment, I found myself looking down upon a tree-lined park, with lots of people leisurely walking about. My attention was particularly drawn to a group of young girls in the distance, strolling arm in arm. I noticed their apparel. They were each dressed in dark gym-slips and very obviously were schoolgirls. I stared upon the scene with amazed awe, because, as aforesaid, I was aware that I was getting a peep into another world, a world that I was aware I was not a part of that I was soon to leave. I was amazed at the similarity of the scene to the world I had left behind in sleep. This new world upon which I gazed was similar to the world in which I belonged, only much more beautiful. Then, it happened! This other world vanished, the school-girls, the park, and the green hill-side. I awoke in my London bed-sitter.

The next few years were troubled, anxious years and had it not been for my awareness of my unseen loved ones constantly with me, life indeed have been desolate and bleak. They were very anxious years because my sister, Shelia, had been suffering with severe depression as a result of my mother's passing, not to mention a broken marriage. She was constantly in and out of hospital, receiving treatment which helped lift the depression temporarily only. She was at home in Ireland during this awful time. Each time she left hospital on arrival home the memories of my mother, enhanced by the sight of my mother's vacant little chair, brought about a relapse in her condition. I wrote each week without fail to her from London comforting her as best I could be relating to her the phenomena that had proved to me beyond doubt that mother had not really left us but was just out of sight until eventually we all meet again. One letter I received from her confirms my belief that my efforts to comfort her were in vain. The quote, "Dear Jo, were it not for your strong convictions about an afterlife I would indeed by in despair. I do believe you when you say you've seen mother and heard her – I do indeed and am much comforted". This knowledge confirmed by her that I was really helping her relieved my anxiety. Gradually she improved, improved so much that she came to join me in London. I introduced her to the British Museum where she joined me to work as a typist. The knowledge that her ability to still work and do a good daily job added greatly to her improvement.

During this period I had what I consider to be a symbolic vision. Today there have been many books written about near-death experiences and those people concerned having been through a long dark tunnel know a great peace and a bright spiritual light awaiting in the distance. This is a common experience today. However, at the time so many years ago when I had this vision I'm about to relate, this phenomenon was unheard of. Yet, as regards my troubled time with my sister, I too experienced this same phenomenon. In my sleep state I found myself in a long dark tunnel, gently and carefully leading my sister by the hand towards a bright inviting light at the end of this tunnel. I then awoke before I reached the light. This vision of guiding my sister towards the light was a sure sign that I was guiding my sister to safety, come what may.

In October 1974 Sheila decided to leave London and return to the little home in Ireland for a holiday. She was magically improved. I left her to the airport, said goodbye to her cheerful, smiling face and returned to my London bed-sitter. But clouds were fast gathering, clouds that neither of us anticipated. In March of the next year, March 16th, I was hurriedly summoned home by my married sister, Madeline. Sheila had all this time been in the best of form, doing a lot of visiting to old friends she had a sudden urge to see. Then came the brain haemorrhage. For over a week she had complained of a bad pain in her head, but, on account of my sister's long history of depression her local doctor did not take serious heed of the pain but said it was 'just nerves'. This doctor had her removed to the local psychiatric hospital where she had been treated for depression through the years. The pain persisted and heed was taken. She was then hurriedly moved to the Royal Hospital in Belfast where a brain scan revealed a haemorrhaging of the brain. On the evening of the 16th march I arrived at her bedside in company with my sister Madeline. When we saw her the pain had ceased and we were surprised and pleased to see her looking quite cheerful. She was tired, though, and rather mixed-up and was under the impression that she was still in the local psychiatric hospital at home. She did not realise how ill she had been. We left her and consulted the neurologist who was attending her. He advised us to try and not worry and assured us that an operation would make her better, stating also that an operation might not even by necessary, that care and rest might clear the trouble. Madeline and I left the hospital feeling greatly relieved and comforted, looking forward to seeing Sheila on the Sunday. And so for a while my sister and I both shed out worry, until a grim warning came to me in the early hours of Sunday morning. At 5.00am that memorable morning, I was awakened from my sleep by a pressure bearing down upon my – the exact same pressure that came upon me in 1960 when by brother, Bennie, appeared before my in my little room in Streatham. As I awoke the pressure lightened but did not lift completely. In my left ear I could hear a whispering voice but it was not clear enough to comprehend. I was fully aware that my mother was with me and kept repeating the question, "Mother, is Shelia going to die?" I asked this question twice for I somehow knew that my mother had come for that reason. As I asked the question I could hear whispering replies. I recall so clearly saying: "Mother, I can't hear you – is Shelia going to die?" Then, strange as it may seem to you, dear reader, clearly I heard her say, "I've come a long way by bus". These words were not said in a whisper but were very, very clear and in my mother's so familiar tone. I ask you, how could I imagine or make up such words as these? I can only say, what can we know of the dimension into which we all go on passing from this world? This statement of my mother's makes me come to the conclusion that the world to which we all pass at death is similar to our physical world. Added to this was the memory of other words, very mementoes, significant words, when, on seeing my mother I asked the question, "mother, this is wonderful, where have you been?" and her reply, "here beside you all the time".

To return to that fateful night, there were further whisperings in my ear and I continued asking the question, "Is Shelia going to die, mother?" Then the whispers ceased the pressure that was upon my lifted completely. I lay feeling very anxious as I knew mother had come to prepare me and that my sister was to leave us. Then, to verify this, around six o'clock it came, the urgent knocking at the front door. It was Madeline, my sister, who said, "Get dressed quickly – we must go to the hospital – Sheila's dying".
We arrived at the hospital in time to see Sheila pass peacefully from this world. I can only hope that when my turn to pass comes, I shall know the peace and

tranquillity that shelia experienced. There was no suffering, no laboured breathing, just a gentle withdrawal. We returned home in sorrow for the loss of our sister but so thankful that she passed away in such peace and without suffering. I kept reflecting on my mother's coming to tell me that Shelia was about to leave us and from this thought I derived much consolation. I was fully convinced that my mother's arms were wide open to receive my sister into her new world. With me still, and always will be, my mother's strange words, "I've come a long way by bus".

The very unique strangest of her words is in itself impressive evidence that I did indeed hear them for no imagination could conjure them up. As I commented previously regarding these words that she had 'come a long way by bus' leaves me with only one conclusion, that conclusion being that the world we all pass to is a similar world to ours, there being transport, roads, distance, etc...

Chapter 9
"Here beside you all the time"

Thereafter, my dearly loved sister, Shelia, in a short space of time after her passing, joined the nightly visitors. The distinction she makes ion the calling of my name to confirm that it is she and not mother who calls is unmistakable. When in this world she was the only member of the family who abbreviated my name, Josephine to 'Jo', whilst mother had always called me "josey', sometimes by my full name Josephine. This abbreviation, this added distinction after Sheila's passing is in itself wonderful evidence that she still lives. So clearly and wisely do they distinguish themselves by their own unique way of calling my name. This in now March 1985 and still they come to me, their voices clearer and stronger than every before. There are periods, perhaps a few weeks, when they do not come. I do miss them and feel very lonely then, but they do come back as they did just a little over a week ago on my sister's anniversary. She returned then to call my name and to let me know she was still with me, as did my mother on 'mother's day' and shelia once again. It is really when I'm in trouble of some kind, feeling low or depressed, that I can rely on them to draw close and make themselves known. For instance, when my darling little dog, Ben, dies my mother called his name so clearly on that distressing night, thus letting me know that she had my little animal companion safe in her care, and so my grief was much eased. There are occasions when I meet those who had known and were fond of Shelia and commented on her passing with tear filled eyes, but I myself had no tears to shed. I had no tears to shed because of my awareness that Shelia was still with me on occasions, visiting from her new world. Always in my mind do I recall my mother's consoling words to me, "here beside you all the time". None know better than I that in God's great creation there is in reality no death, only change into life everlasting. Life is continuous, the circle is unbroken. Often in my childhood I used to ponder on the words of Jesus, "seek and ye shall find". I had felt that these words held the key to a great revelation and I longed to find and to know. Hence I had a special, simple and constant little prayer, 'dear God, help me to understand Thee, help me to find Thee". I consider He has done a lot for me in this direction in answer to this little childish prayer of mine. My little childish plea for enlightenment was answered in later life by the phenomena of the return of my loved ones. The hidden key was turned in the lock when my loved ones came nightly to comfort me and to prove to me the wonderful, glorious truth that life is eternal, that we just pass from this dimension into a higher one. The incident of death is in reality buy change only; we leave the physical body behind, which has served its purpose here. We move on to find that life is unbroken, continuous and gloriously eternal and that we meet our loved ones who have passed on before us.

My conclusions:
The foregoing phenomena have done much more for me than just give me sweet consolation, for through my unusual experiences I received much food for thought about life itself and its purpose for our existence. They have led me to vital conclusions about so-called death and the role this inevitable event plays in life. I am convinced that the incident of death is a necessary part of the pattern of life. In life we are born into this physical world and in death too we are reborn into a higher, more evolved world. I say 'more evolved' because, as I've described to you in this chronicle of

psychic events, I've been there and seen its much greater and more glorious beauty. I have not said 'another life' but continuous life, for the circle of life is unbroken when we leave this earth. This physical world is but a kindergarten in eternity, and we are God's children whose purpose in this world is to learn life's hard lessons in the struggle towards a great and wonderful goal planned for us by our creator, that goal being the soul's perfection. The school of earth is one of very difficult endeavour, frustration and suffering, a life full of challenge and adversity, this challenge and adversity being very necessary for the enfoldment of the soul, for its spiritual evolution. Like the rough diamond that shows forth its inner radiance only by first going through the scorching flames, so too do we find the inner radiance of the soul by going through the purifying fires of life.

Death, the Angel of Light:
For millions of people their understanding of death is totally, sadly wrong, for throughout the ages mankind has looked upon this inevitable event as a terrible finality, separation and great grief. If only they could know the wondrous, joyous truth, if only they knew that the death of the physical body is just the beginning of a wonderful and great adventure of the soul. Death is not an ogre but an Angel of Light, the Gatekeeper to a new and more evolved world, this evolved, more superior world bringing to each soul new and wider horizons, new and greater opportunities. The revelation of this great and wonderful truth was brought to me through the great, caring love of my loved ones who spanned the bridge between our two worlds to come close to me to console and enlighten me to the fact, as my mother so clearly told me, that the dear departed are still close to mankind here on this earth and, to quote her words again, "here beside

you all the time". They brought home to me the fact that death is but an illusion and that all is but change only, change of form upon entry into a new and more evolved environment. Also, I must stress that I myself helped to bring about this closeness of my loved ones, this turning of the key by having, ever since childhood, a very enquiring mind, following the advice of Jesus, "seek and ye shall find". Hence, I sought and have been privileged to find. This anyone can do. Our loved ones cannot come close if we do not want to know, do not seek, and look upon them as gone forever. We must play our part.

Chapter 10
New Form – New Instrument of the Soul

Running throughout all life in this world is a wonderful and mysterious life-force, the life force which, as stated, is eternal, unbroken, and continuous at death. This gloomy word, death, which conjures up dismal thoughts and apprehension, which so terrorises millions of people, will lose its terror when all peoples of the world realise the great truth that this apparently sad event is in reality but the opening of a door to a new and more fulfilling life, when we then understand that it means release from the imprisonment of the flesh and all its accompanying ills, release into another world in a new, more spiritualised form, this new form being a duplicate of the body left behind. Yes, death is but the divesting of heavy, outworn clothing (the earth body), this physical body which we now discard being designed by its creator for use as our instrument in this difficult and very testing environment, the physical world. In death we surrender the coarse, physical atoms and senses of the earth body and find ourselves in possession of its duplicate, the new form, a new instrument for use in a new world, a more evolved body for use in a more evolved world. In death we surrender the outer physical atoms in exchange for a new body of finer and faster vibrating atoms, for use in a higher world of like vibrations.

Vibration:
And now, if I explain the word 'vibration' it may help you understand what I mean regarding this new body and new world just mentioned. Whilst my understanding of science is limited, the little I do know paints for me a picture of all creation as one whole

interpenetration of vibrating, ever-changing energy. Every modern day schoolchild knows that matter is composed of atoms that everything that appears to be static is really not so. The universe and all within it only appears to be static but in reality solidified energy. This energy is in a constant state of motion, of vibrating energy. All forms of life within our universe are attuned to the same vibrating wavelength. Our senses of sight, hearing, touch and smell are attuned to this same wavelength, hence everything appears to us as solid. According to the degree of vibration so is the density of the substance of matter. The life force, mind force, or what we call 'God" is within all creation, within everything from the human, the animal, and down to the hardest mineral, a diamond or iron. This 'God' or supreme power that we look upon as far, far off from us manifests throughout all creation, is continually, eternally manifesting and creating through this wonderful, marvellous process of vibrating, ever-changing energy. This scientific fact is but a small glimpse, and mankind has so much more to discover during his slowly evolving consciousness. Scientists now know that the universe, and all forces of life within it, is in a constant state of motion, a whirling mass of vibrating atoms. The difference in the various forms of life depends upon the degree of vibration, for there are degrees upon degrees of vibration, and, the higher the degree of vibration the higher evolved the creation, the higher evolved the consciousness.

Interpenetration and Duplication:
Interpenetrating this world in which we live is the world to which we all go at death. It is my firm belief that this interpenetrating world is this self-same world as that in which we now live. Also, interpenetrating this higher vibration world are countless other worlds,

myriads of them, hence eternity, worlds full of created life even as we experience it here. Don't ask me how I know, I cannot tell you. I just know and am absolutely convinced of this. All is in a magnificent process of duplicating energy, eternally creating, constantly interchanging. Remember the words of Jesus, "In my Father's house are many mansions". Everything in the vast arena of life is eternally duplicated. There are worlds within worlds, forms within forms. Running throughout is this supreme, grand, super-intelligent, all-knowing, all-creating and mysterious life-force we call 'God', which in our now limited intelligence we do not understand. We can only observe, ponder and wonder at the workings of this supreme mind or super-intelligent power. I would emphasise that our world and all forms of life within it is duplicated by the higher vibration atoms. All forms of life as we know it, both human and animal, are duplicated with countless other sheaths or bodies, all these duplicated sheaths or bodies designed for use as instruments of expression of the Great Spirit that abides within for use in worlds to come, throughout eternity. As I stated earlier, this phase of our lives, this physical world into which we have been born, is but a kindergarten in the school of eternity, a small chapter in the great adventure of life. In future worlds to come there will be new opportunity for the oppressed and those who lacked opportunity here: there is a fresh start for all, even for the foolish and wicked, for the God force manifests within all, however wicked or evil and shall eventually prevail, for this eternity striving for good shall eventually overcome and prevail, perfection always having been the great eternal goal.

Chapter 11
Nothing is wasted:

God is the great mathematician, the supreme planner. Nothing in all His wonderful creation is wasted, not even a corpse. When we pass from this world our outer form, our deceased body, disintegrates and changes into the atmosphere, to be converted into chemicals and eventually re-created into new life. The Spirit of man – of all living things – passes on to the inner and greater dimensional world I've mentioned, where its new sheath or body is now adapted for use in its new world or higher evolved consciousness, for again I repeat, when the Spirit passes on, consciousness also evolves into greater understanding, into new and wondrous revelation. The consciousness of Man carries on into the next dimension with all Life's memories intact and is aware of greater expansion and spiritual power. The world into which the passing soul finds itself is a much more evolved world, hence it is a world of great beauty never before experienced – I know, for I've been there! The consciousness of Man finds new and much greater horizons, much greater wisdom and spiritual understanding.

Nothing Dies:
To animal lovers the world over I say, with full conviction, do not mourn unduly for the little companion you have lost, for nothing dies. As all life is eternal, the little animal you have mourned as gone forever also lives, and also, like man, is enjoying a more evolved and happier life. He too has passed on to the higher world I've mentioned. He too retains his earth memories, retains his memories of you whom he has loved and he awaits reunion with you one day to

continue the joyous companionship he once had with you. His little animal spirit is also in the process of further developing evolvement, for nothing in all God's great creation is wasted. God's purpose for all life is spiritual enfoldment, all within the great scheme of the Creator. The animal, like the human, learns his hard lessons in this Vale of Tears. He too must be compensated for his strivings and his sufferings, and the sufferings of innocent, helpless creatures are all too many... God loves all the creatures of the earth just as much as he loves Man, for He created them also and, what is more, He is within them for they too are God in essence. Again I say, nothing dies, for the eternal essence, the breath of God, is within all, and so all life should be respected for all life is precious in the eyes of the Creator.

Similar World:
It is my conviction that the world that awaits us in similar to this world in which we now live. I believe that the higher worlds which interpenetrated the world we now inhabit are one and the same, the difference being the degree of the creative, vibrating energy which consolidates our two worlds. This higher world is similar to this earth place, for if all life continues – and I know that it does for it has been proved to me that this is so – then it must be similar. In the higher world we all eventually pass to we shall find awaiting us all those who have preceded us, including all life forms that occupied the physical world, all life being eternal with the every-present life force. I am convinced of this, for I have been blessed and privileged to have had glimpses into this higher world! Not only have I seen and clasped my loved ones, but I've seen their environment. I have witnessed the breathtaking beauty of its scenery. I have seen its majestic, blue mountains, its wide, wide roads, its so vivid green

parks, its flowers of wondrous hue, which no flower on this earth can do justice to. I have even trodden the little streets of this higher world – so similar to here, with its busy shoppers walking by. In one of my visitations to this street, when I went searching for my mother, I approached a little lady with a shopping basket in order to question the whereabouts of my mother, but, this little lady, though I stared into her face to speak, failed to see me and just stared blankly through me. You see, I was not yet of her world. As previously detailed, I have seen my darling animals and noted with amazement the loving, excited recognition in their eyes. All this I tell you with such sincere truth, dear reader. I know I seem to have been highly privileged, but you too can be so highly privileged if you take the advice of Jesus who advised, "seek and ye shall find, knock and it shall be opened to you". You will find that the door of truth shall open to you also. It will open to anyone who has the burning desire to know.

The Physical Universe:

I would emphasise that this world in which we now abide is not what is seems to be. Though it appears static it is not really solid at all, for in reality it is a hive of great activity, of constant motion. The common denominator of all physical matter is electrical energy, made up of atoms. All matter; all the solids, liquids and gases that comprise our world and all forms of life therein can be resolved into this common denominator. Scientists know that the atom is not a hardness, solid and indivisible, as hitherto believed, but a vortex of vibrating electricity. Our universe is composed of these vibrating atoms, this electrical energy, hence there is no such thing as solid matter as we know it. The apparently solid matter that we are familiar with, the liquids and gases we know, are all composed of atoms in varying degrees of composition and cohesion – the atoms of each substance having a different assortment of electrons and protons which constitute the atom. Steel, wool, steam, flesh vary only in the composition of their atoms and their degree of cohesion. For example, the atoms from which steel is made vary form the atom of which steam is composed, because of the difference in the grouping of the atoms' protons and electrons. Thus there is no hardness or solidity in matter at all.

Next World – Foundation of our Physical Universe:
Behind and back of all the physical creation what we see is the Spirit World, the Great Reality, the world into which we enter on the change called 'death'. The tendency to think of the next world – which is usually called 'Heaven" – as geographically beyond our world is a fallacy, for the fact is that the apparently empty space that we see is in reality not empty space at all but the world of Spirit, the higher, interpenetrating world. This higher world is the foundation or basis of all manifested matter such as our world. This higher, interpenetrating would is the present physical world in its full reality. This interpenetrating world is the inner and higher dimension of our world, the same world, our present world in all its full reality. What we see with our limited senses is only a pale reflection of things as they really are, of thc universe as it really is. What we regard here as space is in reality the realm of spiritual reality.

Thought:
Thought is the consciousness of God permeating all creation, creating in manifestation of ITSELF, creating in beauty, intelligence and power, creating and re-creating through His highest evolved creation, as far as

we know, Mankind. Thought power is eternally permeating all things, every manifesting the Divine Spirit, the source of all things. Thought is the consciousness of God acting eternally on vibrating energy, in so doing creating the inter-change of energy from one degree of vibration to another. A constant flow of creative thought power travels ever outwards to the vast confines of the Universe, planning the evolution of the Universe and all within it. This constant flow of divine, all-intelligent thought power is so obviously all-intelligent for the Universe, to even the most unobservant eye, is based on law and order. This GREAT THOUGHT, or God, is PURE SPIRIT or LIGHT travelling outward like ripples of a pool when a stone is dropped in. As these thought waves travel outward they slow down in speed. They are made more and more dense until they become the sort of waves or vibrations to which our human senses can respond: in other words, until they reach our physical wavelength. This God-given energy, vibrating at our low physical wavelength, provides us with sensations to which we are accustomed to at birth, sensations which are commonplace to us and which we take for granted. It is only when these thought waves vibrate at our low wavelength that our senses can respond, that we can see ,hear , feel and touch. These same thought waves or energy waves vibrate at the same time on higher vibrations to which our senses cannot respond, as our senses are limited to the wavelength of this world. We cannot see the interpenetration spiritual world, or its inhabitants, because of its higher vibration. The Divine Life Force is forever manifesting, forever creating, forever perfecting ITSELF, the Self in which we and all manifested creation dwell. Remember the words of Jesus: "The Father in Me and I in you".

Now we have seen that in this material plane, or world, the Life Force or energy manifests in the form of physical atoms. We respond to those atoms with our senses provided there are enough atoms in a mass. If, however, like the ripples of a pond we take the vibrating energy before it slows down to our wavelength, we find that this vibrating energy can still be formed into atoms by Divine Creative Thought, but these will be atoms vibrating so fast that our senses cannot respond to them. As mist vanishes with the rising sun, or, as the propeller of an aeroplane is set in motion, the mist, the propeller is still there, they still exist. We cannot see them because they have changed their rate of vibration. Hence we can have a world of atoms with which we have no contact owing to that world's higher vibration. Though our senses cannot see that world it is very real. Human beings are like radio sets – they can only tune in to a fixed vibration, hence our limited senses, our inability to see and hear to interpenetrating Spirit World.

Many Mansions:
Jesus said: "In my House are Many Mansions". His words are scientifically interpreted through the discovery of the vibrating universe. As stated, there are worlds within worlds, dimensions within dimensions. All is duplication. There are forms within forms, all in differing degrees of vibration. Our universe is, as far as we know, on the lowest vibration, thus the physical world is an obstructed universe, obstructed by the denser forms of matter or vibrating cohered atoms. The higher the vibration the more highly evolved the world and the creation within that world. Thus the human, and all life forms, pass at death on to a higher vibrating world and hence to a more higher evolved world, the new body of like

vibration to be used as the soul's instrument in its further enfoldment.

Chapter 12
Unity – All is One:

Just as ice – water and steam are one and the same, thus all creation in being are one – all is one in essence but all, like the ice, water and steam are on different vibrations. All creation, seen and unseen, interpenetrates and is one whole. All is the Divine Force manifesting.

Divine Mind:

As Divine Mind is the creator and governor of all matter on all sheers, or worlds, the higher evolved world is thus a world where the Divine Mind, being in higher degree that in this world of lower vibration, manifests greater power over matter. Thus it is that higher world of Spirit, the interpenetrating world, is a world where thought dominates matter more so than in this physical world of ours. The sufferings of this world are as the result of the lower vibrations of Divine Mind over Matter, and so it is that matter dominates our existence to a very large extent and we have our catastrophes such as earthquakes, floods, etc, not to mention the diseases and ills of the body. Then man leaves this world he finds himself in a world where thought dominates and so he is freed form the adversities and physical set-backs of this earthly existence. Thus, as stated earlier, it seems that the physical world in which we now dwell is a school of experiences, hard experience through adversity, experience which, according to how we react to it, helps the soul's progress for the further progressive stage of its existence in the next world. As thought dominates in the next world, that new life will thus be a life in which disease and pain have no existence.

Also, as the Spirit World is a more highly evolved world, it follows it is a much more beautiful world. To quote the biblical words; "eye hath not seen nor ear heard, nor has it entered into the heart of Man to conceive......" (St. Paul)

God – The Spiritual Essence Within:
God is conscious all-permeating intelligence, power and love. In Him we live and move and have our being. God is within us and without. The God Force is everywhere, nowhere is it not. Closer is He then breathing, nearer than hands and feet. Jesus said: "Go ye into thy closet and pray". When we pray we should direct our prayer within, for God, the eternal Life Force is within – and what can be closer than within. The world that awaits us is also within. Remember the words of Jesus, "The Kingdom of Heaven is within you". So, when we pray we should pray within. We should cultivate a continual awareness of the Divine Life Force within. If we walk through life in constant awareness of God within us, we shall eventually become aware of the reality of His presence and shall realise the peace that passeth understanding. WE shall feel secure and know not worldly fears. The reason for our existence in this physical world of ours is to perfect our soul's progress and eventually return to this great reality from whence we came. Thus we must seek this spiritual reality through constant prayer, simple, trusting, heartfelt prayer. Prayer is simply a 'keeping in touch'. If we constantly keep in touch with the God within us, our understanding of God, of spiritual reality, and the key to a great and wondrous revelation shall be ours. We shall then know the riches the Spirit which has patiently been waiting to be known and the travail and

frustrations of our lives will seem to have been worthwhile and have a meaning for us.

MAN:

Man is God in manifestation, manifesting throughout all creation. Man is a part of the God Force – he is God individualised. He is an eternal spirit, the spiritual essence or life force dwells within him. His physical body is the instrument of his soul which animates it. This spiritual life force within is eternally manifesting and finding expression throughout all creation, embracing all forms of life, including Man, animal, plant, mineral, etc. Man's intelligent mind cannot fail to see that all creation is governed by an over-riding super-intelligent Life Force, a loving, omnipotent, and omniscient, omnipresent ever-at work Intelligence. Working throughout all Nature is this ever-striving creative goal of perfection, a gradual unfolding wonderful process towards perfection, continually effecting away back to the source of origin from whence it came.

Chapter 13
Personality:

As God is the spiritual essence of all things, and, as Mankind is more fully aware and conscience of the God Force with him, he is thus a personalised being, he partaking in his awareness of the great super-intelligent that dominates all. As God is an intelligent life force, it is safe to assume that behind this super-intelligent there is Supreme Mind.

God Realisation:
And so Man is made in the image of God. According to the degrade in which he realises or is aware of the God Force within him, the more evolved a spiritual being he becomes. God manifests more fully in Man and hence he is, unlike the lesser creation, the animal, a thinking and responsible being. I repeat, Man is a part of God and is made in God's image, being endowed with a sense of right and wrong, and, because he is a responsible being, he is therefore accountable for the care and well-being of his lesser brethren, the animal. God must equally love and cherish the lesser of his creation, for the animal is of the God essence also and the animal also is gradually evolving back towards a perfected foal, back to their spiritual source, God.

Evolution or Spiritual Enfoldment:
Man's purpose here on earth is to unfold the God power within him through his strivings through the adverse experiences of this life, for, as hitherto stated, this earth place is but a training school for the soul, a school where the soul, like the worn with the darkness of the earth, its world, is ever groping its way towards the light, to the Godhead from whence it came. God's desire for Man is God- realisation or Self-realisation,

for man to realise the God Force within him, for the more we become aware of this spiritual power within us, the closer we draw to it. The big and wondrous secret is that ALL IS ONE. All is UNITY. God and all within His creation are ONE> it cannot be emphasised too strongly that the the degree that man realises the Divinity within him, the more fully he realises his inherent God, the more fully he becomes aware of Him and the more evolves and the closer he comes to finding his spiritual self.

Awareness:
Man's mind is his gateway to the 'Kingdom of Heaven' of which Jesus spoke. It is through the power of his mind, through the latent, divine power within him, that he becomes aware. "Now we see through a glass darkly – later face to face". (St Paul)
Through the practise of mind control and keen desire for truth and spiritual enfoldment, through concentration on spiritual matters, through the soul's deep desire to know, to find, to seek. Man finds spiritual awareness and fuller understanding of his role and purpose in this physical world, of his ultimate destiny, which is eventual complete union with the Godhead the source of his being. The materialist, the man who is completely wrapped up in the pleasures of this world, the man who does not seek for the source of his being, he will not and cannot find happiness and peace. He may find temporary pleasure, for the world and its temptations has much of this offer, but his pleasures will not last for they are finites, unlike the eternal pleasures of spiritual peace. If man wants peace and happiness, true and lasting, he must seek knowledge of his inner self, the God within him. This is his one and only true way to contentment and security, a way which puts hope in his heart and gives a meaning and purpose to his life here on earth.

Suffering:
As all creation, the universe and all living things within it, is a continual manifestation of God, the God Force thus must suffer with the through His creation. Suffering is necessary in the process of evolution. Suffering is a great teacher, for it stuns the intellect and allows the soul to reach out for God in its cry fro help. The challenge of adversity helps the soul in its climb towards its goal, spiritual perfection. To the extent that we face up to the challenge of suffering, with forbearance and courage, thus do we spiritually evolve and a deeper understanding of life and of others is gained. Through our own trials and heartbreak we understand the suffering of others and hence we can deeply and sincerely sympathise, thus we develop the spiritual qualities within us which, without the experience of adversity we would not have achieved. In its contrast with pleasure suffering affects the growing spirit, as can be understood for the inspired verses below:

"if my days were untroubled and my heart always light,
would I seek that fair land where there is no night,
if I never grew weary with the weight of my load,
would I search for God's peace at the end of the road.
If I never knew sickness and never felt pain,
Would I reach for God's hand to help and sustain.
If I walked not in sorrow and lived without loss,
Would my soul seek sweet solace at the foot of the cross
If all I desired was mine day by day,
Would I kneel to my God and earnestly pray.
If God sent no winter to freeze me with fear
Would I yearn for the warmth of Spring every year.
I tell myself this – and the answer is plain –
If my life were all pleasure and I never knew pain,
I'd seek God less often and need Him much less,
For God's sought more often in times of distress,

And no one knows God or sees Him as Plain
As those who have met Him on the pathway of pain.

(Author unknown)

I came across the above poem many years ago and was very impressed with its great wisdom. No one can deny the truth that these verses contain but they are prevalent with wisdom and tell us that suffering has a vital role to play in the soul's evolution.

Judgment:
There is no personal Judge as orthodox religion so wrongly taught. Man's individual soul is its own judge. When the soul awakens to its new life after the change called 'death' it carries with it all of life's memories, from childhood onwards, all life's experiences which it has undergone. One sees a panorama of all these experiences. It sees its good acts, foolish acts and wicked acts and from this panorama the wisdom of his soul rises and judges itself. It knows deep remorse and shame at its wicked and foolish deeds. It thus reaps spiritual benefit from this judgment upon itself and thus embarks upon a new beginning, a new path in its upward climb towards the divine goal ordained for it. The 'hell' that orthodox teaching has threatened us with is this hell of remorse of the soul. The 'heaven' that men have been told awaits the good is the 'peace that passeth all understanding' which the soul who has led a good life then knows. The Soul's judgment of itself is very necessary for its further evolution in its new life ahead, it sees with a new and clearer vision and hence it gains from the experiences of the life it has left behind.
More Food for Thought:
God is Spirit, essentially abstract yet wonderfully real, revealed throughout all creation. God is Divine Consciousness; God is energy, light, power, love. This

Divine Consciousness is continually manifesting in various forms throughout the universe. Divine energy is the raw material from which God, the Divine Mind, creates the wonders of creation, including ourselves of whose life we are an individual part. The Supreme Life Force, what we call "God" manifests in various forms from the perfect to the imperfect, the imperfect always being on the pathway of enfoldment towards perfection, however long it may take. All creation is Divine Consciousness in essence. All is a gradual stage of evolvement back to the original source of its being, back to the Divine Godhead.

The CHANGE:
There is no such thing as 'death' in the sense of ceasing to exist. There is in reality no death for all is but change of form only. The body disintegrates and dies and returns to the elements from whence it came, but the life force that animated it continues, is unbroken, and is carried on into the new and more superior form, a more evolved form for the new and more evolved life ahead. Science can confirm that throughout the universe all is ceaselessly, everlasting changing. All is progression, nothing is wasted, and nothing in the entire universe dies. All is but change only, change into a higher, and more progressive and evolved life.

Special Meditation:
Consciousness – the supreme Mind of which we as individuals partake – is always the law; it is always the Presence within us; it is always the reality; external things are only the effect, and, as effect cannot be law; as effect cannot be ceased, as effect cannot have power for no effect can have power over another effect. This is spiritual law. Consciousness is all power – consciousness is God. We are GOD individualised. When we come to a full realisation of the God within us,

we come into spiritual power. According to the degree of awareness of the God Consciousness with us, thus the degree of our spiritual advancement or enfoldment of the God Power within us, thus the degree of spiritual peace, the 'peace the passeth all understanding' (Jesus)